Fractions
Are Parts
of Things

Fractions Are Parts of Things

by
J. Richard Dennis

Illustrated by
Donald Crews

Thomas Y. Crowell Company • New York

YOUNG MATH BOOKS

Edited by Dr. Max Beberman,
Director of the Committee on School Mathematics Projects,
University of Illinois

Manufactured in the United States of America
L.C. Card 73-127603
ISBN 0-690-31520-1
0-690-31521-X (Lib. Ed.)
1 2 3 4 5 6 7 8 9 10

Fractions
Are Parts
of Things

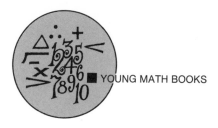 YOUNG MATH BOOKS

You can find one half in lots of places.
You can see one half if you have water and a glass.

one half empty

one half left

one half here

one half here

Sometimes you can see one half if you have a window with a window shade, or a candy bar.

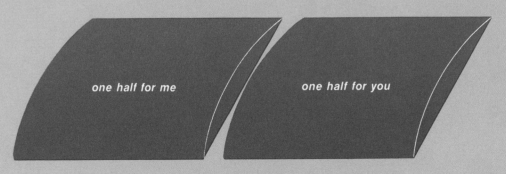

one half for me

one half for you

Often you can see one half in a group of children.

one half have brown hair

one half have black hair

one half are girls

Can you find another way to get one half with these children?

1

You can show one half in many different ways with shapes.

One half with triangles

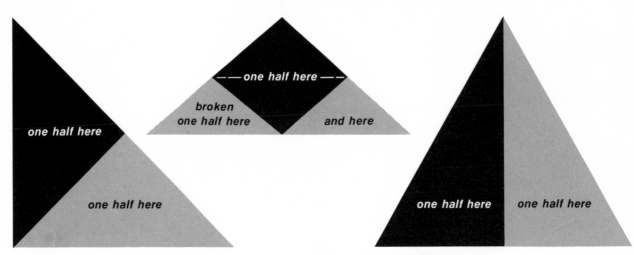

one half here

one half here

—— one half here ——

broken
one half here

and here

one half here

one half here

One half with squares

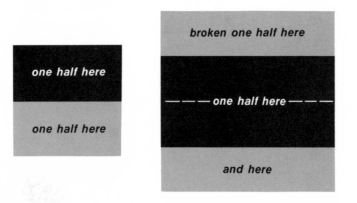

one half here

one half here

broken one half here

— — — one half here — — —

and here

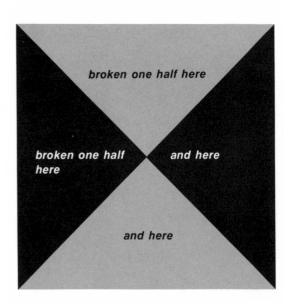

broken one half here

broken one half
here

and here

and here

2

One half with rectangles

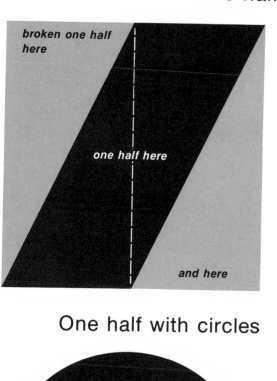

broken one half here

one half here

and here

broken one half here

and here

and one half here

and here — and here

one half here

one half here

One half with circles

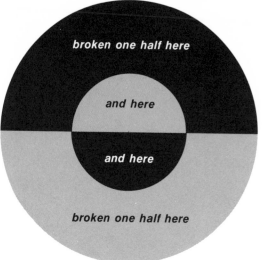

broken one half here

and here

and here

broken one half here

broken one half here

broken one half here

and here

and here

one half here

one half here

3

One half with other shapes

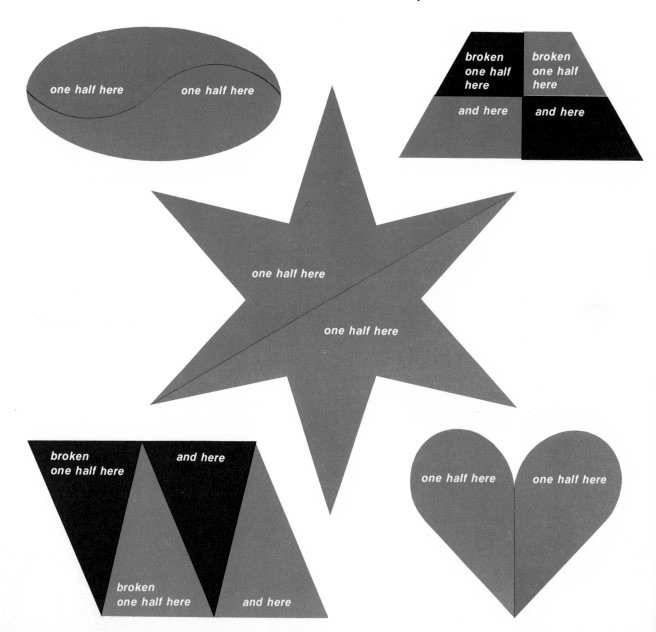

one half here · one half here

broken one half here · broken one half here · and here · and here

one half here · one half here

broken one half here · and here · broken one half here · and here

one half here · one half here

Can you find one half of something in your classroom?
Can you find one half of something at home?

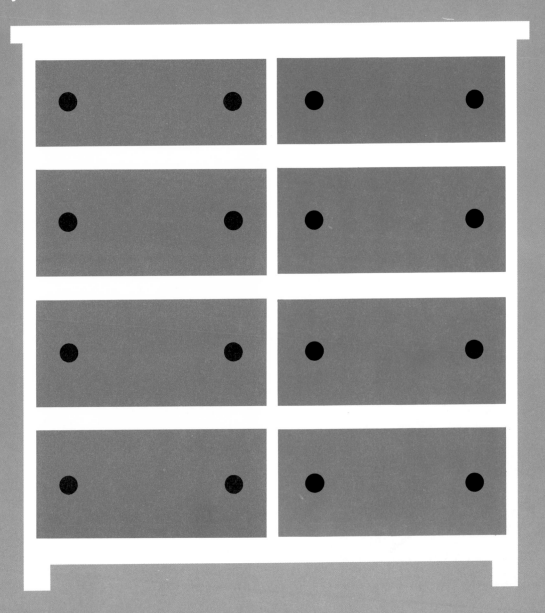

It is easy to see one half in shapes when each half is all in one piece. Sometimes all you need to do is to fold the shape and the halves will match.

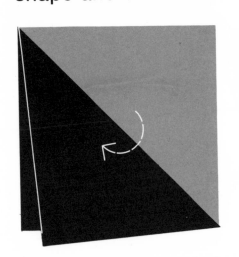

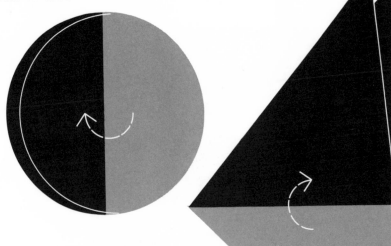

Some broken halves can also be folded together into one piece.

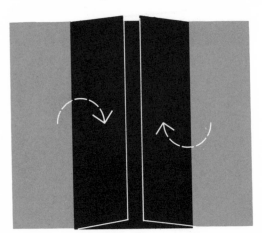

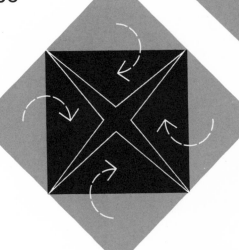

At other times you can cut the halves apart and match them.

7

Cutting and matching the pieces of halves can make
an interesting puzzle.

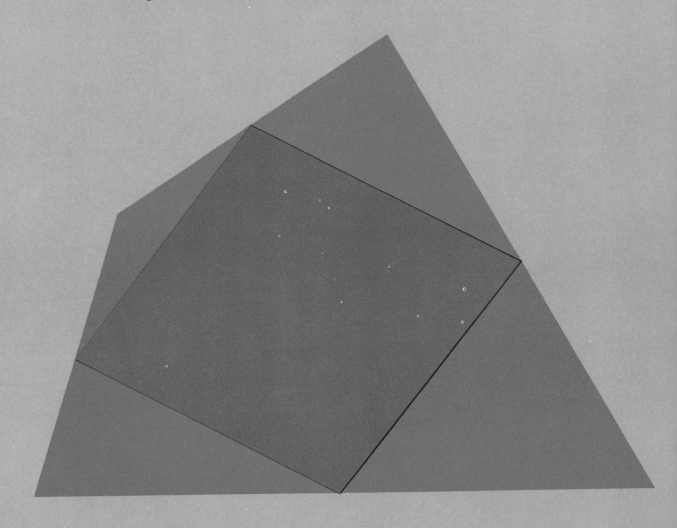

Copy this picture.

An easy way to do this is to trace it.

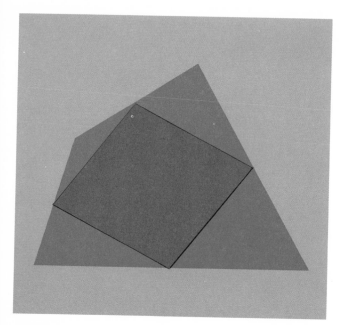

Paste your tracing on a card.

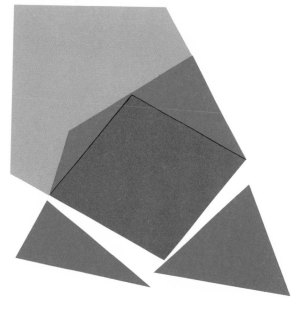

Cut out the blue
and brown pieces.

Now try to fit the brown pieces together on top of the
blue piece.

What am I?

I describe the black part of the circle.

You can also find one third in lots of places.

the shade is pulled down
one third of the way

one third is left

one third for me

12

one third are boys

one third have black hair

one third have blue shirts

13

You can show one third with shapes in many ways.

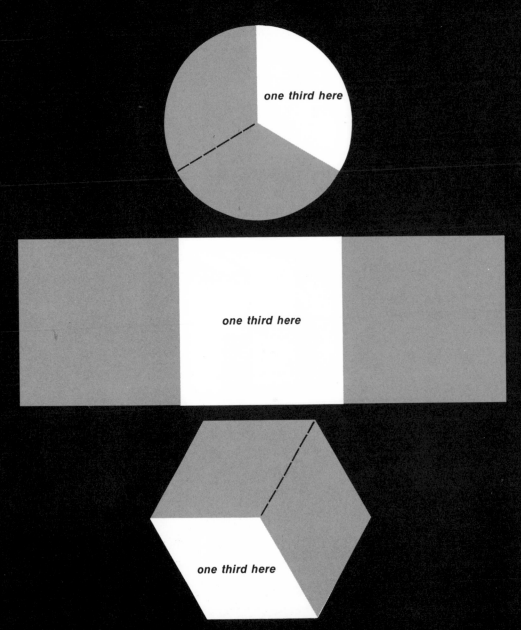

one third here

one third here

one third here

Can you find one third in any other places?

One third always has a partner. When you see one third, you may be able to see two thirds at the same time.

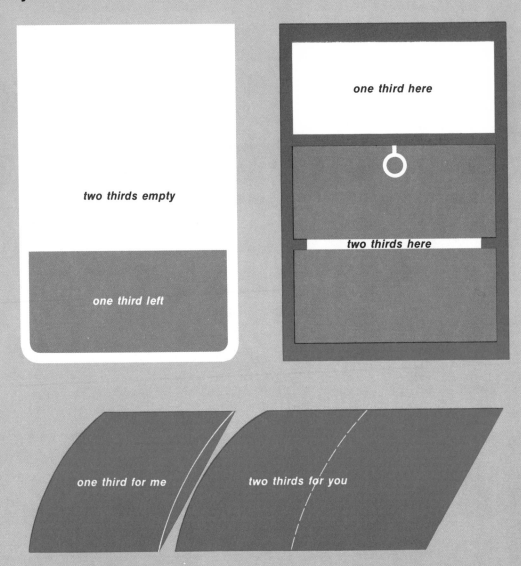

two thirds empty

one third left

one third here

two thirds here

one third for me

two thirds for you

one third are boys   *two thirds are girls*

17

You can show one third and two thirds together in shapes also.

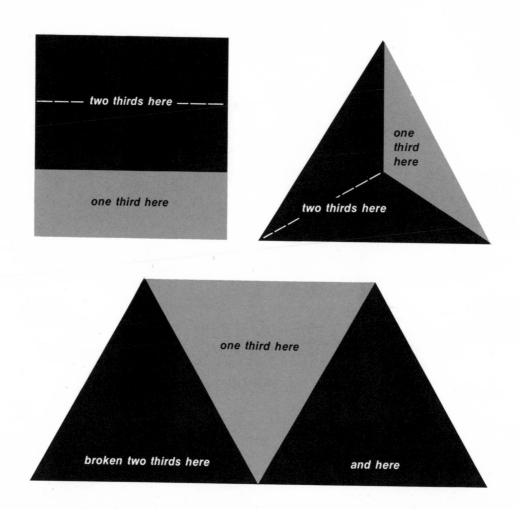

two thirds here

one third here

one third here

two thirds here

one third here

broken two thirds here

and here

Can you find one third of something in your classroom?
Do you find two thirds of it there too?

Take this shape that shows one third and imagine cutting out the one-third piece. This is what you get.

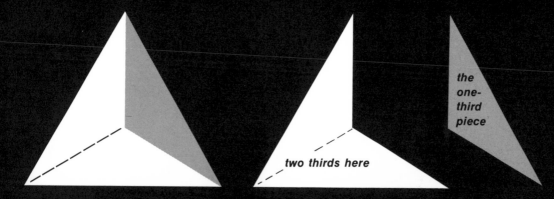

Can you see one half of the two-thirds piece that is left?

Here are some other shapes with the one-third piece cut out.

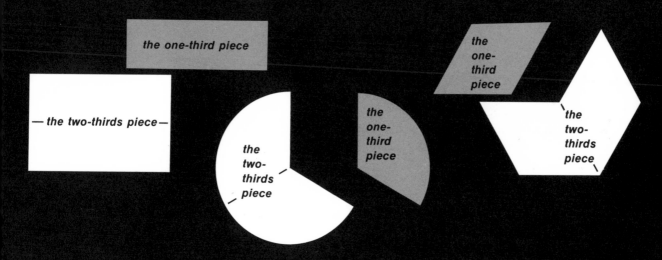

Can you see one half of each of the two-thirds pieces?

19

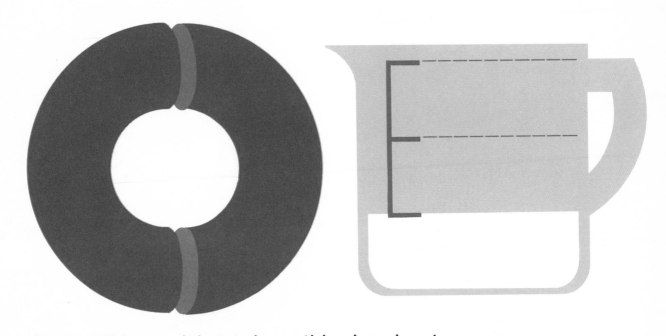

Two children wish to share this doughnut.
How much does each child get?

What am I?
I describe the amount of milk in the cup.

What am I?
I describe the blue part of the kite.
I also describe the black part.

21

What am I?
I describe the black part of the circle.

My partner describes the gray part of the circle.
What is my partner?

You can find one fourth in many places.

One fourth has a partner too. When you find one fourth of
something, you can usually find three fourths of it also.

one fourth are roosters

three fourths are hens

three fourths have sails   *one fourth do not*

25

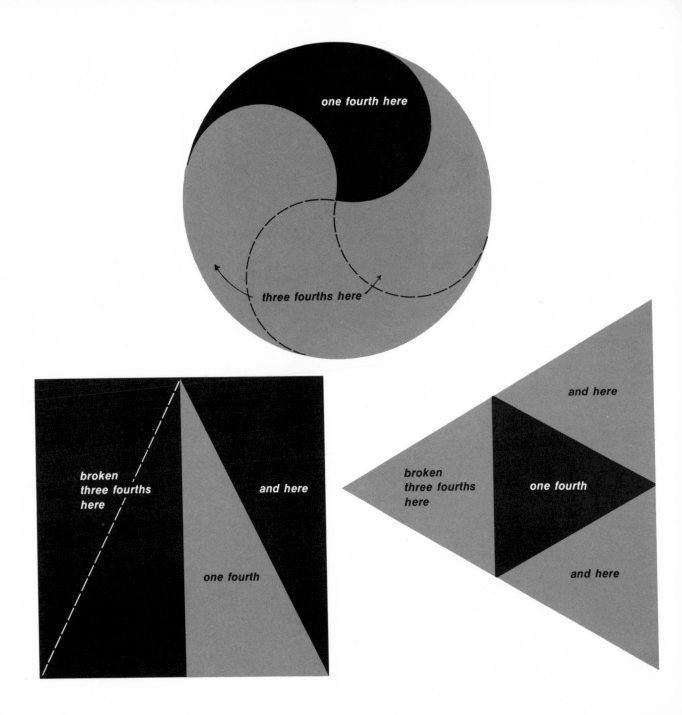

one fourth here

three fourths here

broken
three fourths
here

and here

one fourth

broken
three fourths
here

one fourth

and here

and here

26

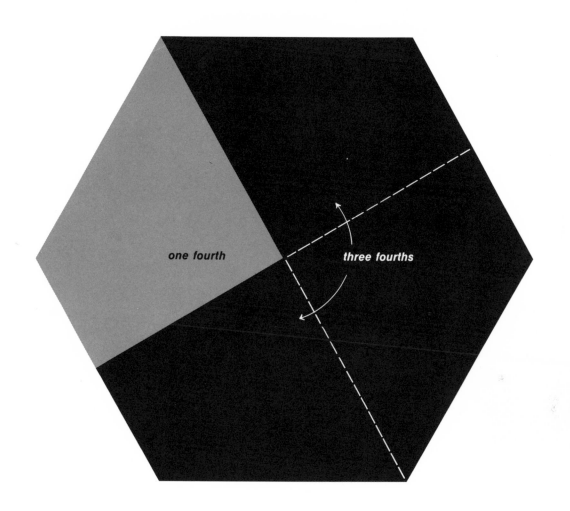

one fourth

three fourths

Can you find one fourth of something in other places?
Is three fourths there too?

Take a shape that shows one fourth
and cut out the one-fourth piece.

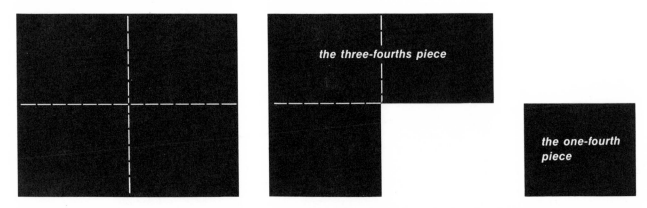

Can you see one third of the three-fourths piece that is left?

Here are some other shapes with a one-fourth piece cut away.

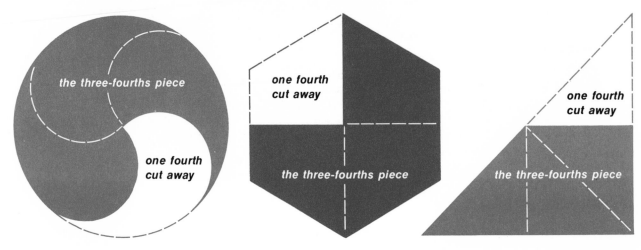

Can you find one third of each of the three-fourths pieces?

What am I?

I describe the blue part of the triangle.

My partner describes the brown part of the triangle.

What is my partner?

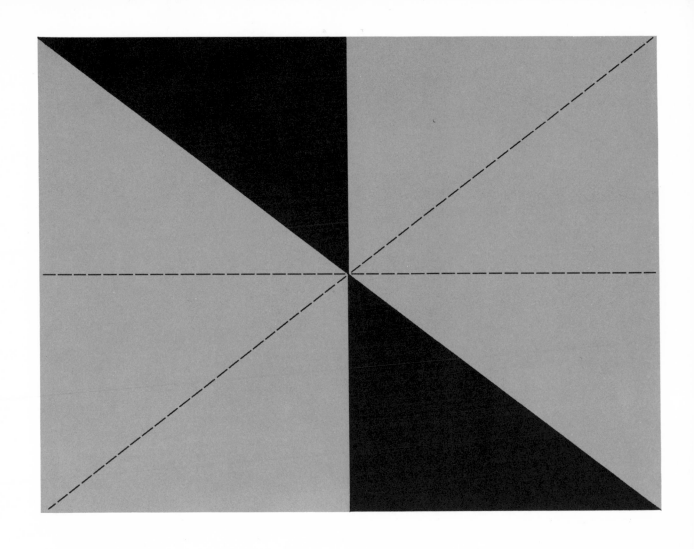

What am I?

I describe the black part.

What is my partner?

I describe the gray part of the square.
What am I?
I also describe the black part.

What am I?
I describe the light gray part of the triangle.
I also describe the dark gray part of the triangle.
And I also describe the black part of the triangle.

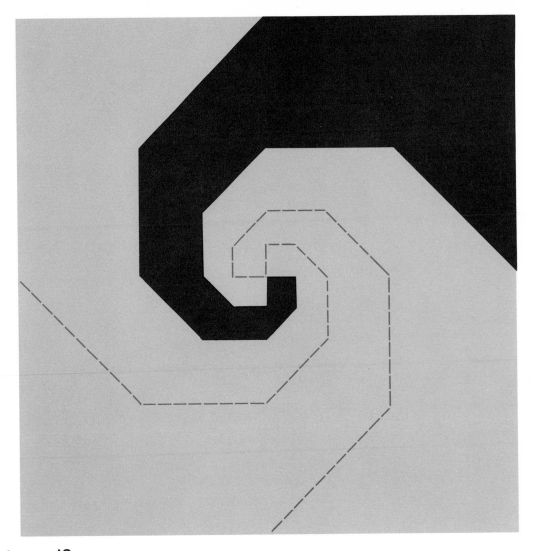

What am I?

I describe the blue part of the square.

My partner describes the black part of the square.

What is my partner?

Watch for us often.

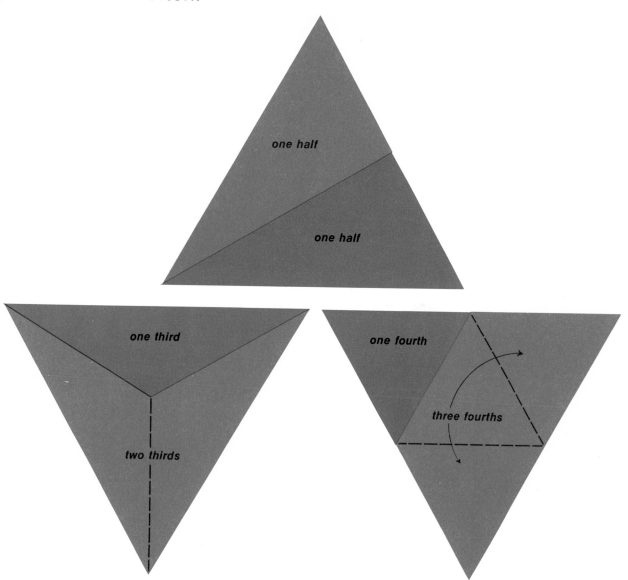

You can find us almost everywhere.

ABOUT THE AUTHOR

Dr. J. Richard Dennis was born and educated in Ohio. He has taught mathematics in Ohio, Indiana, and Illinois, and has been developing mathematics courses and training teachers at the University of Illinois since 1963. He recently completed a stay in Hawaii, where, among other things, he taught a televised course for mathematics teachers. Dr. Dennis is a consulting author for the forthcoming *Heath Mathematics Program,* and coauthor of *Geometry—A Modern Course.*

Fractions Are Parts of Things was a Dennis family project. Mrs. Dennis and each of the three children had a part in creating or clarifying the text. The Dennis family now makes its home in Urbana, Illinois.

ABOUT THE ILLUSTRATOR

Donald Crews is a free-lance designer and photographer, who has his own design office. He works in all areas of graphic design and has written and illustrated several children's books.

He was born in Newark, New Jersey, and is a graduate of New York's Cooper Union for the Advancement of Science and Art. He is married, has two small daughters, and lives and works in New York City.

Mr. Crews' work has appeared in shows at the AIGA and in *Graphis Annual.* His first children's book, *We Read A to Z,* was one of AIGA's 1967 "50 Books of the Year."